Talk To Me In Korean
Workbook
Level 1

written & designed by
TalkToMeInKorean

Talk To Me In Korean Workbook (Level 1)

1판 1쇄	1st edition published	2013. 9. 9
1판 17쇄	17th edition published	2019. 8. 9

지은이	Written by	TalkToMeInKorean
책임편집	Edited by	선경화 Kyung-hwa Sun, 스테파니 베이츠 Stephanie Bates
디자인	Designed by	선윤아 Yoona Sun
삽화	Illustration by	장성원 Sungwon Jang
녹음	Voice Recording by	선경화 Kyung-hwa Sun
펴낸곳	Published by	롱테일북스 Longtail Books
펴낸이	Publisher	이수영 Su Young Lee
편집	Copy-edited by	김보경 Florence Kim
주소	Address	04043 서울 마포구 양화로 12길 16–9(서교동) 북앤빌딩 3층 롱테일북스
		3rd Floor, Book-And Bldg. 16-9, Yanghwa-ro 12-gil, Mapo-gu, Seoul, KOREA
이메일	E-mail	TTMIK@longtailbooks.co.kr
ISBN	978-89-5605-688-3	14710

Talk To Me In Korean Workbook
Level 1

Contents

How to Use
the Talk To Me In Korean Workbook

This workbook is designed to be used in conjunction with the TTMIK Level 1 lessons, which are available for free at www.talktomeinkorean.com. Developed by a certified teacher to help you review and retain what you've learned in the TTMIK lessons, this workbook contains 6 main categories of review and 13 types of exercises:

Categories

1. Vocabulary review
2. Writing
3. Listening comprehension
4. Reading comprehension
5. Fill in the chart
6. Dictation

Types of Exercises

1. Matching
2. Fill in the blank
3. Multiple choice
4. Dictation
5. Draw a picture

6. Translation (Korean <-> English)

7. Short answer

8. Define and translate

9. Conjugation

10. Write your own sentence

11. Q & A

12. Unscramble and write

13. Verbification

The "Dictation" category was designed to aid in the development of Korean listening skills. When you come across the "Dictation" category, you will listen to an audio file of a word or phrase in Korean and write down what you hear. The "Dictation" audio files are available for download in MP3 format at www.talktomeinkorean.com/audio

Romanizations are provided, but we encourage you to refer to our "Quick Guide to 한글 (Hangeul)" to help you learn how to read and write in 한글 (Hangeul). Only relying on romanizations hinders your learning and actually prevents you from becoming better at Korean. So, do yourself a favor and learn 한글 (Hangeul) if you haven't already.

Quick Guide To 한글 (Hangeul)

The Korean alphabet is called 한글 (Hangeul), and there are 24 basic letters and digraphs in 한글.

*digraph: pair of characters used to make one sound (phoneme)

Of the letters, fourteen are consonants (자음), and five of them are doubled to form the five tense consonants (쌍자음).

Consonants

Basic

ㄱ	ㄴ	ㄷ	ㄹ	ㅁ	ㅂ	ㅅ	ㅇ	ㅈ	ㅊ	ㅋ	ㅌ	ㅍ	ㅎ
g/k	n	d/t	r/l	m	b/p	s	ng	j	ch	k	t	p	h
g/k	n	d/t	r/l	m	b/p	s/ɕ	ŋ	dʑ/tɕ	tɕʰ	k/kʰ	t/tʰ	p/pʰ	h

Tense

ㄲ	ㄸ		ㅃ	ㅆ		ㅉ
kk	tt		pp	ss		jj
k'	t'		p'	s'		c'

When it comes to vowels (모음), there are 10 basic letters. 11 additional letters can be created by combining certain basic letters to make a total of 21 vowels. Of the vowels, eight are single pure vowels, also known as monophthongs (단모음), and 13 are diphthongs (이중모음), or two vowel sounds joined into one syllable which creates one sound.

*When saying a monophthong, you are producing one pure vowel with no tongue movement.

*When saying a diphthong, you are producing one sound by saying two vowels. Therefore, your tongue and mouth move quickly from one letter to another (glide or slide) to create a single sound.

Vowels

Monophthongs

ㅏ	ㅓ	ㅗ	ㅜ	ㅡ	ㅣ	ㅐ	ㅔ
a	eo	o	u	eu	i	ae	e
a/a:	ʌ/ə:	o/o:	u/u:	ɨ/ɯ:	i/i:	ɛ/ɛ:	e/e:

Diphthongs

ㅑ	ㅕ	ㅛ	ㅠ		ㅒ	ㅖ
ya	yeo	yo	yu		yae	ye
ja	jʌ	jo	ju		jɛ	je

ㅘ	ㅝ				ㅙ	ㅞ
wa	wo				wae	we
wa	wʌ/wə:				wɛ	we

					ㅚ	ㅟ	ㅢ
					oe	wi	ui
					we	wi	ɨi

* Please refer to the book "한글마스터(Hangeul Master)" for more information.

Writing 한글 letters

한글 is written top to bottom, left to right. For example:

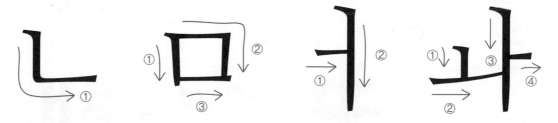

By making sure you follow the stroke order rules, you will find that writing Korean is quite easy and other people will be able to better read your handwriting.

Syllable Blocks

Each Korean syllable is written in a way that forms a block-like shape, with each letter inside the block forming a sound/syllable.

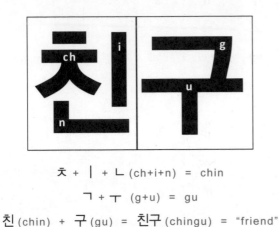

In each syllable block, there is a:

1. * Beginning consonant

2. * Middle vowel

3. Optional final consonant

Required in a syllable block. A block MUST contain a minimum of two letters: 1 consonant and 1 vowel.

ㅊ + ㅣ + ㄴ (ch+i+n) = chin

ㄱ + ㅜ (g+u) = gu

친 (chin) + 구 (gu) = 친구 (chingu) = "friend"

Two of the most common ways to write consonant and vowel combinations in Korean are horizontally and vertically (the boxes drawn here are for illustrative purpose only).

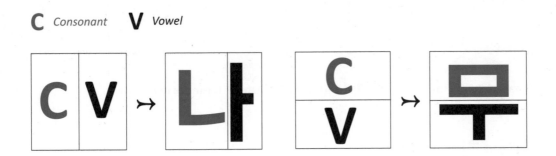

By adding a final consonant (**받침**), the blocks are modified:

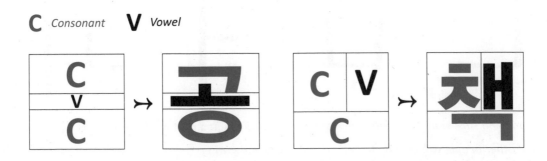

Talk To Me In Korean Workbook

There are also syllables which have two final consonants, such as:

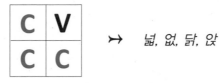

넓, 없, 닭, 앉

In all the syllable blocks, the letters are either compressed or stretched to keep the size relatively the same as the other letters.

Vowels

Since the "minimum two letter" rule exists and one letter has to be a consonant and the other has to be a vowel, what can you do when a vowel needs to be written in its own syllable block? Add the consonant ㅇ [ng] in front of or on top of the vowel. When reading a vowel, such as 아, the ㅇ makes no sound and you just pronounce the ㅏ [a].

*Vowels absolutely, cannot, under any circumstances be written by themselves!!

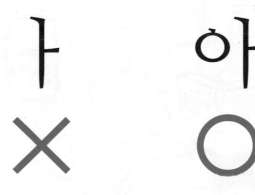

Okay! Now that you are equipped with a basic knowledge of 한글,
it's time to do your part and start practicing!
Let's get to it!

Lesson 1.
Hello, Thank you
안녕하세요, 감사합니다

Section I – Vocabulary

Please define/translate each word in English. Then write it in your preferred language.

1. **존댓말**
   [jon-daen-mal]
   Polite/formal language

2. **안녕**
   [an-nyeong]
   wellbeing, peace, health

3. **하세요**
   [ha-se-yo]
   you do, do you?, please do

4. **안녕하세요**
   [an-nyeong-ha-se-yo]
   Hello

5. **감사**
   [gam-sa]
   appreciation, thankfulness.

6. **합니다**
   [ham-ni-da]
   I do, I am doing

7. **감사합니다**
   [gam-sa-ham-ni-da]
   Thank you

Section II – Writing practice

Saying the syllables and the words aloud as you write them in the spaces below will help you learn faster!

8. **안**
[an]

안 안 안 안 안

9. **녕**
[nyeong]

녕 녕 녕 녕 녕

10. **하**
[ha]

하 하 하 하 하

11. **세**
[se]

세 세 세 세 세

12. **요**
[yo]

요 요 요 요 요

13. **안녕하세요**
[an-nyeong-ha-se-yo]

안녕하세요   안녕하세요

14. **감**
[gam]

감 감 감 감 감

15. **사**
[sa]

사 사 사 사 사

16. **합**
[hap]

합   합   합   합   합

17. **니**
[ni]

니   니   니   니   니

18. **다**
[da]

다   다   다   다   다

19. **감사합니다**
[gam-sa-ham-ni-da]

감사합니다   감사합니다

Section III - Comprehension
Fill-in-the-blank

20. If you want to greet people in the most common way in Korean, you would say: "(안녕하세요   )".

21. When you greet someone by saying, "(안녕하세요   )", that person will most likely respond by saying, "(안녕하세요   )" to you in return.

22. In Korean, if you hear sentences that end in -요 or -니다, it is
[-yo] [-ni-da]
(존댓말   ), or polite/formal language.

23. To thank someone in polite/formal Korean, you should say

"(감사합니다   )".

24. When you write **안녕하세요**, you can write it with a (●) or a (?) at the end. Either one is okay!

Section IV – Dictation

Listen to the corresponding MP3 file. Repeat aloud what you hear, and then write it down. Each word/phrase will be said twice.

You can download the mp3 audio files from:
www.talktomeinkorean.com/ workbookaudio

25. Track 1: 안녕하세요

26. Track 2: 존댓말

27. Track 3: 감사합니다

28. Track 4: 안녕!

Section I – Vocabulary

Match each Korean word to its common English translation.

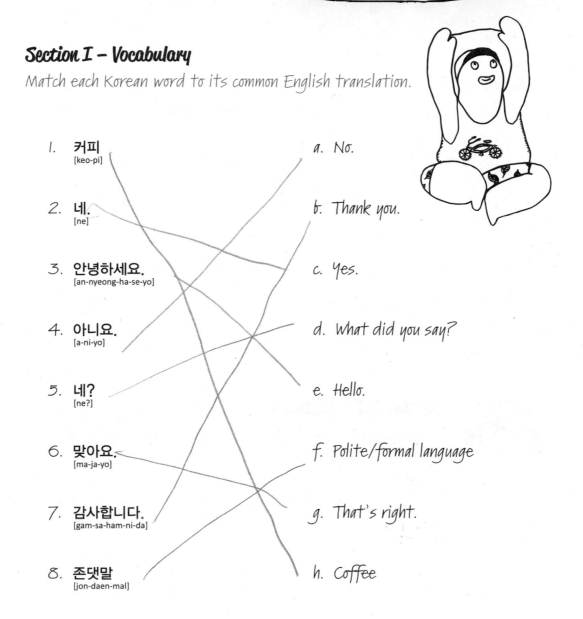

1. 커피
   [keo-pi]

2. 네.
   [ne]

3. 안녕하세요.
   [an-nyeong-ha-se-yo]

4. 아니요.
   [a-ni-yo]

5. 네?
   [ne?]

6. 맞아요.
   [ma-ja-yo]

7. 감사합니다.
   [gam-sa-ham-ni-da]

8. 존댓말
   [jon-daen-mal]

a. No.

b. Thank you.

c. Yes.

d. What did you say?

e. Hello.

f. Polite/formal language

g. That's right.

h. Coffee

Section II - Comprehension
Fill-in-the-blank

9. The word (네) is a very versatile word and can mean many things, such as "I see", "Ah-ha", "I got it", "I understand"...etc.

10. By saying "(아니요)", you are expressing your disagreement or denial to what the other person said.

11. To clearly express that you are listening and not just nodding and passively listening, you would say "(맞아요)".

12. Both 네 and 아니요 are in (존댓말), or polite/formal
[ne]   [a-ni-yo]
language.

Section III - Dictation
Listen to the corresponding MP3 file. Repeat aloud what you hear, and then write it down. Each word/phrase will be said twice.

13. Track 5: 아니요

14. Track 6: 네. 맞아요

Talk To Me In Korean Workbook

15. Track 7: 녀?

Section IV – Writing Practice

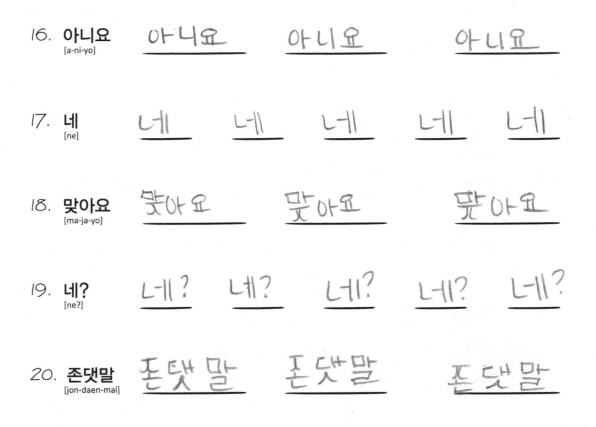

16. **아니요** 아니요   아니요   아니요
[a-ni-yo]

17. **네** 네   네   네   네   네
[ne]

18. **맞아요** 맞아요   맞아요   맞아요
[ma-ja-yo]

19. **네?** 네? 네?   네?   네? 네?
[ne?]

20. **존댓말** 존댓말   존댓말   존댓말
[jon-daen-mal]

Lesson 3. Goodbye, See you
안녕히 가세요, 안녕히 계세요, 안녕

Section I - Vocabulary

Multiple choice. Circle the best answer.

1. **존댓말** means:
   [jon-daen-mal]

   a. Hello

   b. Polite/formal language

   c. Thank you

   d. TTMIK is awesome!

2. "Go in peace" is the English translation for the greeting:

   a. **맞아요**
   [ma-ja-yo]

   b. **안녕히 가세요**
   [an-nyeong-hi ga-se-yo]

   c. **안녕**
   [an-nyeong]

   d. **아니요**
   [a-ni-yo]

3. What does **안녕** translate to in English?
   [an-nyeong]

   a. Television

   b. Orange

   c. Well-being; peace; health

   d. Thank you

20   Talk To Me In Korean Workbook

4. 네 can be used to mean:
   [ne]

    a. Yes

    b. That's right/correct

    c. I understand

    (d.) All of the above

5. What is the Korean expression that you would use if you were the one leaving, and the other person is staying?

    a. **안녕**
    [an-nyeong]

    b. **안녕하세요**
    [an-nyeong-ha-se-yo]

    c. **안녕히 가세요**
    [an-nyeong-hi ga-se-yo]

    (d.) **안녕히 계세요**
    [an-nyeong-hi gye-se-yo]

Section II - Unscramble and Write

6. **요하녕세안.**
(yo-ha-nyeong-se-an)

안녕하세요

7. **니합감사다.**
(ni-hap-gam-sa-da)

감사합니다

8. **요가녕히안세.**
(yo-ga-nyeong-hi-an-se)

안녕히 가세요

9. **세계요히녕안.**
(se-gye-yo-hi-nyeong-an)

안녕히 계세요

Section III - Comprehension

Multiple choice. Circle the best answer.

10. When Koreans say 안녕하세요, 안녕히 계세요, and 안녕히 가세요, they
[an-nyeong-ha-se-yo] [an-nyeong-hi gye-se-yo]   [an-nyeong-hi ga-se-yo]
don't always pronounce every single letter clearly. Often you end up only

hearing:

 a. 안녕
    [an-nyeong]
 b. 하
    [ha]
 c. 가요
    [ga-yo]
 d. 세요
    [se-yo]

11. If you are leaving and the other person is staying, you are literally telling

the other person to "stay in peace" by saying:

 a. 안녕하세요
    [an-nyeong-ha-se-yo]
 b. 안녕히 가세요
    [an-nyeong-hi ga-se-yo]
 c. 안녕히 계세요
    [an-nyeong-hi gye-se-yo]
 d. 감사합니다
    [gam-sa-ham-ni-da]

12. If both you and the other person are leaving at the same time, you would

say, " (   ) " to each other:

 a. 안녕히 계세요
    [an-nyeong-hi gye-se-yo]
 b. 존댓말
    [jeon-daen-mal]
 c. 안녕히 가세요
    [an-nyeong-hi ga-se-yo]
 d. 감사합니다
    [gam-sa-ham-ni-da]

13. Who is more fun to listen to?

    a. **현우**
       [hyeo-nu]

    b. **경은**
       [gyeong-eun]

    c. Both of them are equally fun

    d. I don't like either one of them!

14. If the Korean word for "go" is **가다**, then (   )
                                       [ga-da]
literally means "go in peace".

    a. **커피**
       [keo-pi]

    b. **안녕히 가세요**
       [an-nyeong-hi-ga-se-yo]

    c. **네**
       [ne]

    d. **맞아요**
       [ma-ja-yo]

Section IV – Writing Practice

15. **안녕히 가세요**
[an-nyeong-hi ga-se-yo]
    안녕히 가세요   안녕히 가세요

16. **안녕히 계세요**
[an-nyeong-hi gye-se-yo]
    안녕히 계세요   안녕히 계세요

17. **안녕하세요**
[an-nyeong-ha-se-yo]
    안녕하세요   안녕하세요

Section V - Dictation

Listen to the corresponding MP3 file. Repeat aloud what you hear, and then write it down. Each word/phrase will be said twice.

18. Track 8:

안녕히 계서요!

19. Track 9:

안녕히 가서요!

20. Track 10:

안녕하서요!

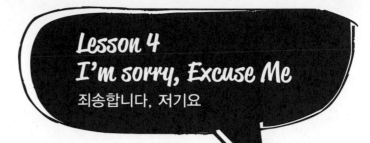

Lesson 4
I'm sorry, Excuse Me
죄송합니다, 저기요

Section I – Vocabulary

Please define/translate each word in English. Then write it in your preferred language.

1. **감사**
   [gam-sa]
   thankfulness, appreciation

2. **합니다**
   [ham-ni-da]
   I do

3. **죄송**
   [joe-song]
   apology, being sorry, feeling ashamed

4. **죄송합니다**
   [joe-song-ham-ni-da]
   I am sorry, I apologize

5. **저기요**
   [jeo-gi-yo]
   over there, excuse me

6. **잠깐만요**
   [jam-kkan-man-nyo]
   Just a second

7. **잠시만요**
   [jam-si-man-nyo]
   Just a second

8. Why does 합니다 sound like it is pronounced "ham-ni-da"? Use the space
[ham-ni-da]
below to write your answer.

you are'nt separating the words and its closer
and makes 9 smooth transition to ㄴ/ (ni)
so the ㅂ is pronounces softer like an ㅁ (m).

9. There are 2 basic situations in which 저기요 can be used. Write them below.
[jeo-gi-yo]
— when trying to get someone's attention

— Or call a waiter in a resturant.

10. 죄송합니다 translates to "I'm sorry". Can you also use it when you want to
[joe-song-ham-ni-da]
say "I am sorry to hear that"? Why or why not?

No because its used as like I apologize your not
the one apologizing for what happened because
you didn't do anything.

11. There are 3 ways to say "excuse me" when you want to pass through a
crowd. Write them below.

1. 저 기 요, (Jeo-gi-yo)

2. 잠시만요 (a jam-si-man-yo)

3. 잠 깐만 요 (jam-kkan-man-yo)

12. When you want to get someone's attention in order to talk to them by saying "excuse me" in Korean, you should say:

    a. **죄송합니다**
       [joe-song-ham-ni-da]
    b. **안녕하세요**
       [an-nyeong-ha-se-yo]
    c. **저기요**
       [jeo-gi-yo]
    d. **커피**
       [keo-pi]

Section III - Dictation

Listen to the corresponding MP3 file. Repeat aloud what you hear, and then write it down. Each word/phrase will be said twice.

13. Track 11:

저 기요

14. Track 12:

죄송합니다

15. Track 13:

잠시만요

16. Track 14:

잠깐만요

Section IV - Draw!

17. Draw a picture or write a story/poem/song/ whatever you want in your native language that will help you remember when to use 죄송합니다, 저기요,
[joe-song-ham-ni-da] [jeo-gi-yo]
잠깐만요, and 잠시만요.
[jam-kkan-man-nyo] [jam-si-man-nyo]

♪ Everyday when your walking down the street ♪ you sometimes accidently bump into someone, "oops! I'm sorry" (죄송합니다) OR your on the train and your shoes untied so you ask them to wait a sec. "Just a sec!" (잠깐만요 and 잠시만요). Wne you get off your stop. You go to a resturant and you eat amazing food so you ~~ask~~ call the waiter for the check, "Excuse me!" (저기요)

THE END.

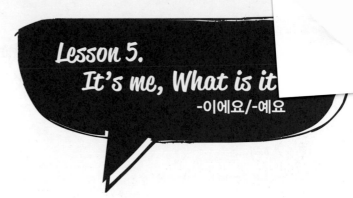

Section I - Vocabulary

Please define/translate each word in English. Then write it in your preferred language.

1. **가방:**
   [ga-bang]:

2. **물:**
   [mul]:

3. **사무실:**
   [sa-mu-sil]:

4. **학교:**
   [hak-gyo]:

5. **저:**
   [jeo]:

6. **뭐:**
   [mwo]

Section II - Translation and Writing Practice

Write the phrase in Korean on the given lines. Say the phrase in Korean aloud as you write it!

7. It's a bag.

_____   _____   _____

8. What is it?

_____   _____   _____

9. It's me.

_____   _____   _____

10. Is this water?

_____   _____   _____

11. It's an office.

_____   _____   _____

Section III – Comprehension
Fill-in-the-blank

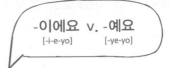

12. If the last letter of the previous word ends in a consonant, you should use
"(   )".

13. If the last letter of the previous word ends in a vowel, you should use
"(   )".

14. Both of these endings have a similar role to that of the English verb
"(   )".

True/False

15. 이에요 and 예요 have different meanings. _____
    [i-e-yo]   [ye-yo]

16. 맞아요 means "Thank you". _____
    [ma-ja-yo]

17. If you mix up 이에요 and 예요, it's not a big deal. _____
            [i-e-yo]   [ye-yo]

18. I want to talk to 현우 in Korean, not 경은. _____
                    [hyeo-nu]   [gyeong-eun]

19. When using 이에요 or 예요, you are using 존댓말, or
[i-e-yo]   [ye-yo]   [jon-daen-mal]
polite/formal language.

_____

20. The Korean word for "coffee" is 물. _____

Section IV - Dictation

Listen to the corresponding MP3 file. Repeat aloud what you
hear, and then write it down. Each word/phrase will be said
twice.

21.   Track 15:

22. Track 16:

23. Track 17:

24. Track 18:

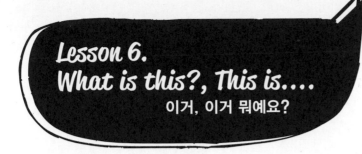

Lesson 6.
What is this?, This is....
이거, 이거 뭐예요?

Section I - Vocabulary

Match each Korean word to its common English translation.

1. **뭐**
   [mwo]

2. **책**
   [chaek]

3. **사전**
   [sa-jeon]

4. **핸드폰**
   [haen-deu-pon]

5. **카메라**
   [ka-me-ra]

6. **이거**
   [i-geo]

7. **저**
   [jeo]

a. This (thing)

b. Cell phone

c. What

d. I, Me

e. Book

f. Camera

g. Dictionary

Section II - Comprehension

Match each picture with the corresponding word.

8.

9.

10.

11.

12.

a. 책
[chaek]

b. 물
[mul]

c. 카메라
[ka-me-ra]

d. 핸드폰
[haen-deu-pon]

e. 사전
[sa-jeon]

Section III - Writing

Write a short conversation between two people, one person asking "What is this?" and the other giving an answer.

Section IV - Dictation

Listen to the corresponding MP3 file. Repeat aloud what you hear, and then write it down. Each word/phrase will be said twice.

13. Track 19:

14. Track 20:

15. Track 21:

16. Track 22:

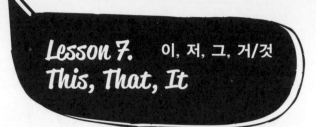

Lesson 7.
This, That, It
이, 저, 그, 거/것

Section I - Vocabulary

Match each Korean word to its best English translation.

1. **이것**
   [i-geot]

   a. the person; that person; he; she

2. **그 사람**
   [geu sa-ram]

   b. that thing over there

3. **저것**
   [jeo-geot]

   c. this person; this man here;
      this lady here; he, she

4. **저 사람**
   [jeo sa-ram]

   d. this thing; this item; this one

5. **그것**
   [geu-geot]

   e. the thing; the item; that one; it

6. **이 사람**
   [i sa-ram]

   f. that person over there; he;she

Section II - Comprehension

Fill-in-the-blank

이 or 저 or 그
[i]   [jeo]   [geu]

7.   Generally, when you are referring to something farther away from you and closer to the other person you are talking to, you use the word "(   )".

8.   Generally, when you are referring to something near yourself, you use the word "(   )".

9.   Generally, when you are referring to something far away from both you and the other person you are talking with, you use the word "(   )".

Section III - Writing

Translate each word/phrase to Korean.

10.   that cell phone over there =

11.   the camera =

12.   this book =

13.   this bag =

14.   that school over there =

15.   the office =

Lesson 8.
It's NOT me 아니에요

Section I - Vocabulary

Please define/translate each word in English, then write it in your preferred language (if not English).

1. **우유:**
    [u-yu]
    _____

2. **물:**
    [mul]
    _____

3. **고양이:**
    [go-yang-i]
    _____

4. **학생:**
    [hak-saeng]
    _____

5. **모자:**
    [mo-ja]
    _____

6. **것/거:**
    [geot/geo]
    _____

7. **아니에요:**
    [a-ni-e-yo]
    _____

8. **이:**
    [i]
    _____

9. **그:**
    [geu]
    _____

10. **저:**
[jeo]

_____

 ## Section II - Translation practice
Translate each word/phrase to Korean.

11. Hello. =

12. That (over there) is not a cat. =

13. Thank you. =

14. This is not coffee. =

15. Yes, I am a student. =

16. Goodbye! (to the person leaving) =

17. What is this? =

18. No. This is an office. =

19. It is not a cell phone. =

20. Yes, that's right. This is milk. =

Section III - Comprehension

21. How do you say "it's not me" in Korean?

    a. 우유 아니에요.
       [u-yo a-ni-e-yo.]

    b. 감사합니다.
       [gam-sa-hap-ni-da.]

    c. 물이에요.
       [mu-ri-e-yo.]

    d. 저 아니에요.
       [jeo a-ni-e-yo.]

22. If you are having a conversation with someone, and they ask, "이거 모자예요?", while pointing to something near to them, pick one of the following responses that correctly answers the question:

    a. 저거 모자 아니에요.
       [jeo-geo mo-ja a-ni-e-yo.]

    b. 이거 모자 아니에요.
       [i-geo mo-ja a-ni-e-yo.]

    c. 그거 모자 아니에요.
       [geu-geo mo-ja a-ni-e-yo.]

    d. 뭐?!
       [mwo?!]

23. What is the Korean word for "milk"?

    a. 물   *c.* 커피
       [mul]   [keo-pi]

    b. 우유   *d.* 고양이
       [u-yu]   [go-yang-i]

24. The structure of Korean sentences is a bit different in English. For example, in English you would say "this is not a book", but if you were to say, "이거 책 아니에요" in Korean, the literal (word for word) English translation would be:

a. This book not is.

b. Not is this book.

c. This is not book.

d. Book is not this.

Section IV - Dictation

Listen to the corresponding MP3 file. Repeat aloud what you hear, and then write it down. Each word/phrase will be said twice.

25. Track 23:

26. Track 24:

27. Track 25_ver2:

28. Track 26:

Lesson 9. Topic and Subject Marking Particles
-은/는, -이/가

Section I - Vocabulary

1. 내일 translates to what English word?
   [nae-il]

   a. Today

   b. Yesterday

   c. Tomorrow

   d. Forever alone

2. What is the Korean word for "bag"?

   a. 우유
      [u-yu]

   b. 고양이
      [go-yang-i]

   c. 안녕하세요
      [an-nyeong-ha-se-yo]

   d. 가방
      [ga-bang]

3. 사과 is (   ) in English.
   [sa-gwa]

   a. Apple

   b. Pear

   c. Pineapple

   d. Rambutan

4. "Orange juice" is _____ in Korean.

    a. 경은
       [gyeong-eun]
    b. 커피
       [keo-pi]
    c. 오렌지 주스
       [o-ren-ji ju-seu]
    d. 물
       [mul]

5. The Korean word for "today" is:

    a. 저기요
       [jeo-gi-yo]
    b. 날씨
       [nal-ssi]
    c. 뭐?!
       [mwo?!]
    d. 오늘
       [o-neul]

6. 날씨 translates to what English word?
   [nal-ssi]

    a. Weather

    b. Today

    c. Tomorrow

    d. Coffee

7. What is the Korean word for "It's good" or "I like it"?

    a. 학교
       [hak-gyo]
    b. 감사합니다
       [gam-sa-ham-ni-da]
    c. 좋아요
       [jo-a-yo]
    d. 고양이
       [go-yang-i]

8. 학교 is (   ) in English.
   [hak-gyo]

    a. "It's good" / "I like it"

    b. School

    c. Orange juice

    d. Bag

Section II - Writing practice

Write the following words with the correct topic/subject marking particles.

9. 저 (은/는): _____
   [jeo]

10. 오렌지 주스 (은/는): _____
    [o-ren-ji ju-seu]

11. 내일 (은/는): _____
    [nae-il]

12. 가방 (은/는): _____
    [ga-bang]

13. 물 (이/가): _____
    [mul]

14. 학교 (이/가): _____
    [hak-gyo]

15. 고양이 (이/가): _____
    [go-yang-i]

16. 사무실 (이/가): _____
    [sa-mu-sil]

Section III - Comprehension

Complete the translation by just adding topic/subject marking particles to an appropriate place in the given sentences.

*The weather is good today. = 오늘 날씨 좋네요.
[o-neul nal-ssi jot-ne-yo.]

*This book is good. = 이 책 좋아요.
[i chaek jo-a-yo.]

17. The weather hasn't been so good lately, but TODAY, it's good.

=

18. Today, not necessarily everything else, but at least the weather is good.

=

19. The other books are not good, and I don't care about the other books. At least this book is good.

=

20. No other [book] besides this book is good. Someone might have asked me which book is good, and I want to say this one is good compared to other books.

=

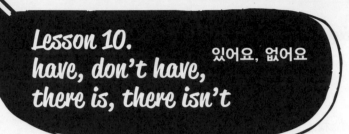

Lesson 10.
have, don't have, there is, there isn't
있어요, 없어요

Section I - Vocabulary

Please define/translate each word in English. Then write it in your preferred language!

1. **친구:**
   [chin-gu]
   _____

2. **시간:**
   [si-gan]
   _____

3. **재미:**
   [jae-mi]
   _____

4. **물:**
   [mul]
   _____

5. **없다:**
   [eop-da]
   _____

6. **있다:**
   [it-da]
   _____

Section II - Comprehension

In Korean, please provide short answers to the following questions.

7. **친구 있어요?**
   [chin-gu i-sseo-yo?]

8. Is TTMIK fun?

9. If you want to imply that you have other things, but TIME is not something you have, you can say:

10. If someone asks you "What is it that you don't have?" and you want to say that time is what you don't have, you can say:

11. Translate this sentence into Korean: "As for friends, I don't have any."

Use English and your preferred language to answer the following questions:

12. What is the difference between " - 이에요 " and " 있어요 "?
          [-i-e-yo]   [i-sseo-yo]

13. What is the difference between " 아니에요 " and " 없어요 "?
          [a-ni-e-yo]   [eop-sseo-yo]

Section III - Dictation

Listen to the corresponding MP3 file. Repeat aloud what you hear, and then write it down. Each word/phrase will be said twice.

14. Track 27:

15. Track 28:

16. Track 29:

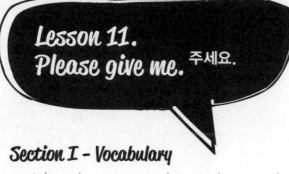

Lesson 11.
Please give me. 주세요.

Section I - Vocabulary

Match each Korean word to its best English translation.

1. **밥**
   [bap]

2. **햄버거**
   [haem-beo-geo]

3. **아이스크림**
   [a-i-seu-keu-rim]

4. **사과**
   [sa-gwa]

5. **돈**
   [don]

6. **커피**
   [keo-pi]

7. **시간**
   [si-gan]

8. **오렌지**
   [o-ren-ji]

9. **맥주**
   [maek-ju]

10. **장갑**
    [jang-gap]

a. ice cream

b. orange

c. glove

d. time

e. beer

f. steamed rice; food; meal

g. hamburger

h. coffee

i. money

j. apple

Section II – Practice exercises

Fill-in-the-blank

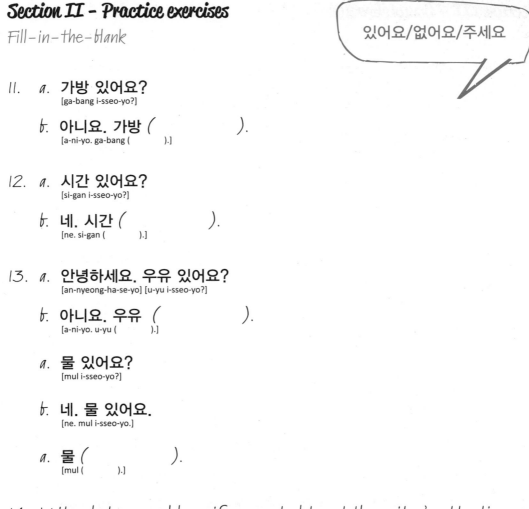

있어요/없어요/주세요

11. a. **가방 있어요?**
       [ga-bang i-sseo-yo?]

    b. **아니요. 가방 (   ).**
       [a-ni-yo. ga-bang (   ).]

12. a. **시간 있어요?**
       [si-gan i-sseo-yo?]

    b. **네. 시간 (   ).**
       [ne. si-gan (   ).]

13. a. **안녕하세요. 우유 있어요?**
       [an-nyeong-ha-se-yo] [u-yu i-sseo-yo?]

    b. **아니요. 우유 (   ).**
       [a-ni-yo. u-yu (   ).]

    a. **물 있어요?**
       [mul i-sseo-yo?]

    b. **네. 물 있어요.**
       [ne. mul i-sseo-yo.]

    a. **물 (   ).**
       [mul (   ).]

14. Write what you would say if you wanted to get the waiter's attention and order a coffee.

    (   )

15. Ask a shop attendant if he/she has any oranges.

    (   )

16. How can you make a sentence into a question when you are speaking?

    a. By raising the tone at the end of the sentence.

    b. By screaming at the top of your lungs like a fangirl.

    c. By whispering.

    d. By speaking while your mouth is full of food.

17. Is there a strict distinction between plural and singular nouns in Korean?

    a. Yes

    b. No

    c. I don't know

    d. 경은 is really pretty!
      [gyeong-eun]

18. It is important to remember that in English, when you ask someone to give you something like juice, the sentence is said as, "Please give me an orange juice." In Korean, it's said as "오렌지 주스 주세요", which literally means
[o-ren-ji ju-seu ju-se-yo]
(   ).

    a. Orange juice

    b. Orange juice please give me

    c. Please give me orange juice

    d. Orange give juice me please

19. **주세요** comes from the Korean verb (   ).
[ju-se-yo]

    a. **가다**
         [ga-da]

    b. **하다**
         [ha-da]

    c. **주다**
         [ju-da]

    d. **나다**
         [na-da]

20. **주다** literally means (   ).
[ju-da]

    a. To give

    b. To do

    c. To go

    d. Peace and well-being

21. Literally, **주세요** means (   ).
[ju-se-yo]

    a. Goodbye

    b. Hyunwoo is really awesome.

    c. Hello

    d. Please give

22. **주세요** is in (   ), or polite/formal language, regardless
[ju-se-yo]

of to whom it is said or who says it.

    a. **감사합니다**
         [gam-sa-ham-ni-da]

    b. **안녕하세요**
         [an-nyeong-ha-se-yo]

    c. **안녕히 가세요**
         [an-nyeong-hi ga-se-yo]

    d. **존댓말**
         [jon-daen-mal]

23. **주세요** can be used in which of the following situations:
[ju-se-yo]

a. When you ask someone to hand something over to you

b. When you are ordering something at a restaurant

c. When you are asking for an item in a shop

d. When attached to a verb in order to ask someone to do something for you

e. All of the above

 ## Section IV – Dictation

Listen to the corresponding MP3 file. Repeat aloud what you hear, and then write it down. Each word/phrase will be said twice.

24. Track 30:

25. Track 31:

26. Track 32:

27. Track 33:

Talk To Me In Korean Workbook

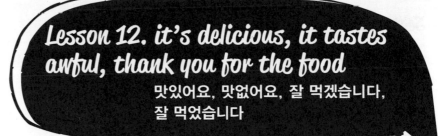

Lesson 12. it's delicious, it tastes awful, thank you for the food

맛있어요, 맛없어요, 잘 먹겠습니다, 잘 먹었습니다

Section I - Vocabulary

Please define/translate each word in English. Then write it in your preferred language!

1. **김밥**
   [gim-bap]
   _____

2. **맛**
   [mat]
   _____

3. **잘**
   [jal]
   _____

4. **케이크**
   [ke-i-keu]
   _____

5. **뭐;무엇**
   [mwo; mu-eot]
   _____

6. **굴**
   [gul]
   _____

7. **치킨**
   [chi-kin]
   _____

8. **삼겹살**
   [sam-gyeop-sal]
   _____

Section II - Writing practice

9. 잘 먹겠습니다. – I will eat well.
[jal meok-ge-sseum-ni-da]

_____   _____   _____

10. 맛있어요. – It's delicious.
[ma-si-sseo-yo]

_____   _____   _____

11. 맛없어요. – It tastes awful.
[ma-deop-sseo-yo]

_____   _____   _____

12. 잘 먹었습니다. – I have eaten well.
[jal meo-geo-sseum-ni-da]

_____   _____   _____

13. 잘 먹을게. – Thank you for treating me.
[jal meo-geul-kke]

_____   _____   _____

Section III - Comprehension

True/False - If the statement is false, correct the underlined word or phrase to make it true.

14. Once you have finished a meal, and you want to thank someone for the meal, you can use the expression 잘 먹겠습니다.
[jal meok-ge-sseum-ni-da]

»

15. If you want to thank your friend for treating you to a meal before you eat, you would use the expression 잘 먹을게!
[jal meo-geul-kke]

»

16. 잘 means "taste" in Korean.
[jal]

»

17. If you want to say "This cake is delicious" in Korean, you would say "김치 주세요."
[gim-chi ju-se-yo]

»

18. 맛있어요 is pronounced "mat-i-sseo-yo."

»

19. "I am going to eat well" or "I will eat well" is <u>잘 먹겠습니다</u> in Korean.
[jal meok-ge-sseum-ni-da]

   ››

20. If something does not taste good, is not tasty, or it simply tastes awful,
you can say "<u>맛없어요.</u>"
[ma-deop-sseo-yo]

   ››

Section IV - Dictation
Listen to the corresponding MP3 file. Repeat aloud what you
hear, and then write it down. Each word/phrase will be said
twice.

21. Track 34:

22. Track 35:

23. Track 36:

24. Track 37:

Lesson 13.
I want to... -고 싶어요

Section I - Vocabulary

Match each Korean word to its most common English translation.

1. **가다**
   [ga-da]

2. **보다**
   [bo-da]

3. **먹다**
   [meok-da]

4. **햄버거**
   [haem-beo-geo]

5. **회**
   [hoe]

6. **돈**
   [don]

7. **더**
   [deo]

a. Money

b. To eat

c. Thinly sliced raw fish

d. More

e. To go

f. Hamburger

g. To see

Section II - Writing
Translate each word/phrase to Korean

8. I want to eat. =

9. I want to go. =

10. I want to see/look/watch. =

11. It's delicious. =

12. I will eat well. =

13. Please give me more. =

14. I want to eat more! =

Talk To Me In Korean Workbook

Section III - Comprehension
Fill-in-the-blank

15. 보고 싶어요 has 2 meanings. One literally means "I want to see", and the
[bo-go si-peo-yo]
other means "(   )" in English.

16. To change a verb into the -고 싶어요 form, you just drop the (   )
[-go si-peo-yo]
(the last letter in all Korean verbs in the infinitive form) and add -고 싶어요.
[-go si-peo-yo]

17. In English, you would say "I want to eat more", but in Korean, you literally
are saying "More eat want" when you use the phrase (   ).

Section IV - Dictation
Listen to the corresponding MP3 file. Repeat aloud what you
hear, and then write it down. Each word/phrase will be said
twice.

18. Track 38:

19. Track 39:

20. Track 40:

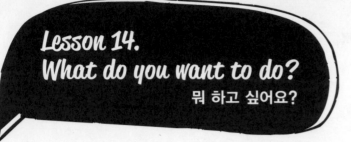

Lesson 14.
What do you want to do?
뭐 하고 싶어요?

Section I - Vocabulary

Please define/translate each word in English. Then write it in your preferred language!

1. **하다**
    [ha-da]
    _____

2. **보다**
    [bo-da]
    _____

3. **먹다**
    [meok-da]
    _____

4. **사다**
    [sa-da]
    _____

5. **마시다**
    [ma-si-da]
    _____

6. **뭐**
    [mwo]
    _____

7. **텔레비전**
    [tel-le-bi-jeon]
    _____

8. **읽다**
    [ik-da]
    _____

9. **자다**
    [ja-da]
    _____

10. 놀다
[nol-da]
_____

11. 쉬다
[swi-da]
_____

12. 일하다
[i-ra-da]
_____

Section II - Comprehension

Answer the following questions by using the prompts in parenthesis in your response, then translate each sentence to English and your preferred language (if not English).

Ex.

가방 사고 싶어요? (네)
[ga-bang sa-go si-peo-yo?] [ne]

Answer : 네. 가방 사고 싶어요. = Yes, I want to buy a bag.

13. 텔레비전 보고 싶어요? (네)
[tel-le-bi-jeon bo-go si-peo-yo?] [ne]

Answer :

14. 이거 뭐예요? (모자)
[i-geo mwo-ye-yo?] [mo-ja]

Answer :

15. 뭐 하고 싶어요? (케이크, 먹다)
[mwo ha-go si-peo-yo?] [ke-i-keu] [meok-da]

Answer :

16. 뭐 보고 싶어요? (뉴스)
[mwo bo-go si-peo-yo?]   [nyu-seu]

Answer :

17. 더 마시고 싶어요? (네)
[deo ma-si-go si-peo-yo?]   [ne]

Answer :

18. 뭐 하고 싶어요? (놀다)
[mwo ha-go si-peo-yo?]   [nol-da]

Answer :

Section III - Dictation
Listen to the corresponding MP3 file. Repeat aloud what you hear, and then write it down. Each word/phrase will be said twice.

19. Track 41:

20. Track 42:

21. Track 43:

Lesson 15.
Sino-Korean Numbers

일, 이, 삼, 사...

Section I - Vocabulary

Match each Korean number to its corresponding digit.

1. **팔**
   [pal]

2. **오**
   [o]

3. **일**
   [il]

4. **륙** or **육**
   [ryuk]   [yuk]

5. **구**
   [gu]

6. **삼**
   [sam]

7. **이**
   [i]

8. **사**
   [sa]

9. **십**
   [sip]

10. **칠**
    [chil]

11. **백**
    [baek]

12. **천**
    [cheon]

a. 100

b. 1

c. 2

d. 3

e. 4

f. 1,000

g. 5

h. 6

i. 7

j. 8

k. 9

l. 10

Section II - Writing

Write out each number using Sino-Korean numbers. Saying the numbers aloud in Korean will make it easier to remember!

Ex.

75:    칠십오
       [chil-ssi-bo]

13. 54: _____

14. 98: _____

15. 67: _____

16. 11: _____

17. 24: _____

18. 100: _____

19. 574: _____

20. 343: _____

21. 999: _____

22. 123: _____

23. 1000: _____

24. 4392: _____

25. 6815: _____

26. 9999: _____

27. 7829: _____

Section III - Dictation

Listen to the corresponding MP3 file. Each number is a Sino-Korean number and will be said twice. Please write your answer as an Arabic numeral (1,2,3,4,5...etc.)

28. Track 44:

29. Track 45:

30. Track 46:

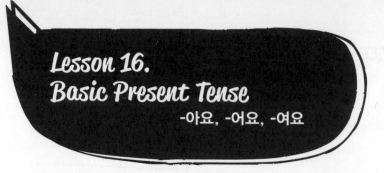

Lesson 16.
Basic Present Tense
-아요, -어요, -여요

Section I - Vocabulary

Please define/translate each word in English. Then write it in your preferred language!

1. **가다**
   [ga-da]
   _____

2. **먹다**
   [meok-da]
   _____

3. **자다**
   [ja-da]
   _____

4. **때리다**
   [ttae-ri-da]
   _____

5. **웃다**
   [ut-da]
   _____

6. **놀다**
   [nol-da]
   _____

7. **보이다**
   [bo-i-da]
   _____

8. **일하다**
   [i-ra-da]
   _____

9. 사무실
[sa-mu-sil]

_____

10. 돈
[don]

_____

Section II - Comprehension
Fill-in-the-blank

11. If the verb stem's last vowel is (   ) or (   ), it is followed by **아요**.
[a-yo]

12. Only one verb stem, which is (   ), is followed by **여요**.
[yeo-yo]

13. **하다** becomes (   ) in the present tense, and it means "I do", "you
[ha-da]
do", "he does", or "they do".

14. If the verb stem's last vowel is NOT (   ) or (   ), it is followed by
어요.
[eo-yo]

15. Over time, **하** + **여요** became (   ).
[ha] [yeo-yo]

16. **봐요** used to be written and pronounced as (   ).
[bwa-yo]

17. **–아요**, **–어요**, and **–여요** are in (   ), or polite/formal language.
    [-a-yo]   [-eo-yo]   [-yeo-yo]

Section III - Writing

Turn these infinitive verbs (verbs that are in dictionary form) into present-tense form.

18. **놀다**   ⟶
    [nol-da]

19. **웃다**   ⟶
    [ut-da]

20. **없다** *(to not exist)*   ⟶
    [eop-da]

21. **오다** *(to come)*   ⟶
    [o-da]

22. **받다** *(to receive)*   ⟶
    [bat-da]

23. **살다** *(to live)*   ⟶
    [sal-da]

Talk To Me In Korean Workbook

Section IV - Dictation

Listen to the corresponding MP3 file. Repeat aloud what you hear, and then write it down. Each word/phrase will be said twice.

24. Track 47:

25. Track 48:

26. Track 49:

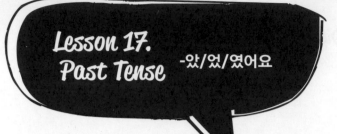

Lesson 17.
Past Tense -았/었/였어요

Section I - Vocabulary

Please define/translate each word in English. Then write it in your preferred language!

1. **멋있다**
    [meo-sit-da]
    _____

2. **이상하다**
    [i-sang-ha-da]
    _____

3. **기다리다**
    [gi-da-ri-da]
    _____

4. **쓰다**
    [sseu-da]
    _____

5. **놀다**
    [nol-da]
    _____

6. **팔다**
    [pal-da]
    _____

7. **먹다**
    [meok-da]
    _____

8. **하다**
    [ha-da]
    _____

9. **적다**
    [jeok-da]
    _____

10. **오다**
    [o-da]
    _____

11. **사다**
    [sa-da]
    _____

Section II - Fill in the chart

Fill in the chart with the verbs in 존댓말.
[jon-daen-mal]

Infinitive (Dictionary Form)	Present Tense	Past Tense
Ex. 가다 [ga-da]	가요	갔어요
12. 잡다 [jap-da]		
13. 먹다 [meok-da]		
14. 팔다 [pal-da]		
15. 쓰다 [sseu-da]		
16. 기다리다 [gi-da-ri-da]		
17. 이상하다 [i-sang-ha-da]		

18. 놀다 [nol-da]		
19. 하다 [ha-da]		
20. 사다 [sa-da]		
21. 오다 [o-da]		
22. 멋있다 [meo-sit-da]		

Section III - Comprehension

True/False – If the statement is false, correct the underlined word or phrase to make it true.

23. You drop the <u>verb stem</u> from any verb in the infinitive (dictionary) form and add 았어요 or 였어요.
[a-sseo-yo]   [yeo-sseo-yo]

    »

24. Verb stems ending with vowels ㅗ or ㅏ are followed by 아요 in the present
[o]   [a]   [a-yo]
tense, and 았어요 in the past tense.
[a-sseo-yo]

    »

25. The verb 하다 is followed by 았어요 in the past tense.
[ha-da] [a-sseo-yo]

   »

26. 샀어요 translates to "I ate/you ate/he ate/they ate/she ate..etc".
[sa-sseo-yo]

   »

Section IV - Dictation
Listen to the corresponding MP3 file. Repeat aloud what you hear, and then write it down. Each word/phrase will be said twice.

27. Track 50:

28. Track 51:

29. Track 52:

Lesson 18.
Location Marking Particles
에, 에서

Section I - Vocabulary

1. The Korean word for "where" is:

    a. 이

    b. 가

    c. 어디

    d. 는

2. -에 means:

    a. I want to go somewhere.

    b. At, to

    c. Person

    d. Hyunwoo still does not have friends.

3. This particle is used to make a location, a time, a situation, and many other things.

    a. -이

    b. -가

    c. -은

    d. -에

4. The English translation for 가다 is:
   [ga-da]

   a. To go

   b. To sleep

   c. School

   d. To write

5. –에서 expresses:
   [-e-seo]

   a. The topic of a sentence

   b. A location where an action is taking place

   c. The meaning of "from" a place

   d. Both b and c.

6. How do you say "now" in Korean?

   a. 학교
      [hak-gyo]

   b. 지금
      [ji-geum]

   c. 어디에 있어요?
      [eo-di-e i-sseo-yo?]

   d. None of the above

7. The Korean word for "office" is:

   a. 가방
      [ga-bang]

   b. 돈
      [don]

   c. 사무실
      [sa-mu-sil]

   d. 집
      [jip]

8. 집 means:
    [jip]

    a. Office

    b. School

    c. Work

    d. Home

Section II – Writing

Use either 에 or 에서 to fill in the blanks. Then translate each sentence to English and your preferred language.

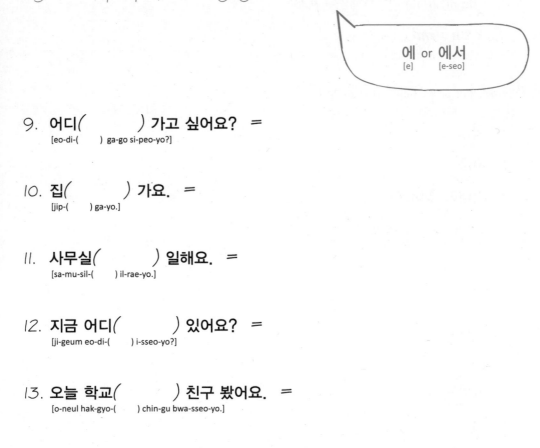

에 or 에서
[e]   [e-seo]

9. 어디(   ) 가고 싶어요? =
    [eo-di-(   ) ga-go si-peo-yo?]

10. 집(   ) 가요. =
    [jip-(   ) ga-yo.]

11. 사무실(   ) 일해요. =
    [sa-mu-sil-(   ) il-rae-yo.]

12. 지금 어디(   ) 있어요? =
    [ji-geum eo-di-(   ) i-sseo-yo?]

13. 오늘 학교(   ) 친구 봤어요. =
    [o-neul hak-gyo-(   ) chin-gu bwa-sseo-yo.]

Section III - Comprehension

Based on the conversation below, answer questions 14-17.

A: 어디 가요?
[eo-di ga-yo?]

B: 학교에 가요.
[hak-gyo-e ga-yo.]

A: 학교에서 뭐 해요?
[hak-gyo-e-seo mwo hae-yo?]

B: 책을 읽어요.
[chae-geul il-geo-yo.]

A: 현우 씨도 학교 가요?
[hyeo-nu ssi-do hak-gyo ga-yo?]

B: 아니요. 현우 씨는 사무실에 가요.
[a-ni-yo. hyeo-nu ssi-neun sa-mu-si-re ga-yo.]

14. Where is Person B going?

15. What will Person B do?

16. Person A asks if Hyunwoo is going to (   )

17. Hyunwoo is actually going to (   )

Section IV - Dictation

Listen to the corresponding MP3 file. Repeat aloud what you hear, and then write it down. Each word/phrase will be said twice.

18. Track 53:

19. Track 54:

20. Track 55:

Lesson 19. When
언제

Section I - Vocabulary

Please define/translate each word in English. Then write it in your preferred language!

1. **도착하다**
   [do-cha-ka-da]
   _____

2. **일어나다**
   [i-reo-na-da]
   _____

3. **오늘**
   [o-neul]
   _____

4. **어제**
   [eo-je]
   _____

5. **내일**
   [nae-il]
   _____

6. **지금**
   [ji-geum]
   _____

7. **아까**
   [a-kka]
   _____

8. **나중에**
   [na-jung-e]
   _____

Section II - Comprehension

Fill-in-the-blank

9. Unlike (   ), to which you have to add location marking parti-

cles to specify, 언제 can be used on its own.

[eon-je]

10. (   ) means "when", while **어제** means "(   )."

[eo-je]

Section III - Writing

Write a simple sentence in the past tense using 언제 and the prompt in parenthesis.

[eon-je]

11. (가다)

[ga-da]

12. (사다)

[sa-da]

13. (도착하다)

[do-cha-ka-da]

14. (일하다)

[i-ra-da]

Talk To Me In Korean Workbook

Write a simple sentence in the present tense using 언제 and the prompt in
parenthesis.
[eon-je]

15. (일하다)
   [i-ra-da]

16. (일어나다)
   [i-reo-na-da]

17. (학교에 가다)
   [hak-gyo-e ga-da]

Answer the following questions in Korean by using any word found in Section I.

18. 언제 사무실에 왔어요?
   [eon-je sa-mu-si-re wa-sseo-yo?]

19. 언제 일해요?
   [eon-je i-rae-yo?]

20. 언제 학교에 도착했어요?
   [eon-je hak-gyo-e do-cha-kae-sseo-yo?]

Section IV – Dictation

Listen to the corresponding MP3 file. Repeat aloud what you hear, and then write it down. Each word/phrase will be said twice.

21. Track 56:

22. Track 57:

Lesson 20. 하나, 둘, 셋, 넷...
Native Korean Numbers

Section I - Vocabulary

Match each Korean number to its corresponding digit.

1. 예순넷
[ye-sun-net]

    a. 47

2. 일흔다섯
[i-reun-da-seot]

    b. 1001

3. 하나
[ha-na]

    c. 56

4. 열아홉
[yeo-ra-hop]

    d. 64

5. 이백다섯
[i-baek-da-seot]

    e. 83

6. 스물둘
[seu-mul-dul]

    f. 95

7. 쉰여섯
[swin-nyeo-seot]

    g. 205

8. 천하나
[cheo-na-na]

    h. 18

9. 여든셋
[yeo-deun-set]

    i. 75

10. 아흔다섯
[a-heun-da-seot]

    j. 1

11. 열여덟
[yeol-lyeo-deol]

    k. 19

12. 마흔일곱
[ma-heu-nil-gop]

    l. 22

Section II - Comprehension

Fill in the chart with the appropriate Korean number

Arabic numeral	Sino-Korean Number	Native Korean Number
Ex. 2	이	둘
1. 33		
2. 100		
3. 80		
4. 96		
5. 71		
6. 20		
7. 92		
8. 68		
9. 11		
10. 44		
11. 1004		

Section III - Let's Count!

Write your answers to the questions using Native Korean numbers.

12. How many **사람** are in this photo?
    [sa-ram]   _____

13. How many dishes are in this photo?   _____

14. How many **강아지** (puppy) are in this photo?
    [gang-a-ji]   _____

Section IV - Dictation

Listen to the corresponding MP3 file. Each number is a Sino-Korean number and will be said twice. Please write your answer as an Arabic numeral (1,2,3,4,5...etc.)

15. Track 58:

16. Track 59:

17. Track 60:

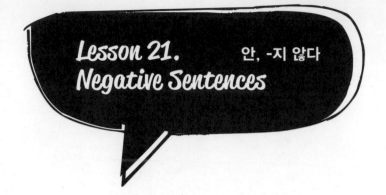

Lesson 21.
Negative Sentences

안, -지 않다

Section I - Vocabulary

Please define/translate each word in English. Then write it in your preferred language!

1. 버리다
[beo-ri-da]
_____

2. 맵다
[maep-da]
_____

3. 먹다
[meok-da]
_____

4. 배고프다
[bae-go-peu-da]
_____

5. 가다
[ga-da]
_____

6. 아프다
[a-peu-da]
_____

7. 집
[jip]
_____

8. 아직
[a-jik]
_____

Section II - Comprehension

Answer the following questions.

9. There are two ways to make negative sentences in Korean. Which method is commonly used in more formal situations, but not always?

10. Of the two ways to make negative sentences in Korean, which method is commonly used in everyday situations and to friends?

Answer the following questions by using a negative sentence structure.

Ex.

학교에 가요?
[hak-gyo-e ga-yo?]

아니요, 학교에 안 가요.
[a-ni-yo, hak-gyo-e an ga-yo.]

11. 김밥이 매워요?
[kim-ba-bi mae-wo-yo?]

12. 케이크 먹었어요?
[ke-i-keu meo-geo-sseo-yo?]

13. 집에 가요?
[ji-be ga-yo?]

14. 그거 버렸어요?
[geu-geo beo-ryeo-sseo-yo?]

15. 아파요?
[a-pa-yo?]

Section III - Fill in the chart

Verbs in 존댓말.
[jon-daen-mal]

Infinitive (dictionary form)	Negative form in present tense (simple and more colloquial)	Negative from in present tense (relatively formal)
Ex. 가다 [ga-da]	안 가요	가지 않아요
16. 마시다 [ma-si-da]		
17. 먹다 [meok-da]		
18. 버리다 [beo-ri-da]		
19. 아프다 [a-peu-da]		
20. 일어나다 [i-reo-na-da]		
21. 자다 [ja-da]		
22. 놀다 [nol-da]		

23. 하다 [ha-da]		
24. 사다 [sa-da]		
25. 보다 [bo-da]		
26. 멋있다 [meo-sit-da]		

Section IV - Dictation

Listen to the corresponding MP3 file. Repeat aloud what you hear, and then write it down. Each word/phrase will be said twice.

27. Track 61:

28. Track 62:

29. Track 63:

Section I - Vocabulary

Write the translation/definition in English. Then write it in your preferred language.

1. **공부**
   [gong-bu]
   _____

2. **일**
   [il]
   _____

3. **기억**
   [gi-eok]
   _____

4. **청소**
   [cheong-so]
   _____

5. **요리**
   [yo-ri]
   _____

6. **이사**
   [i-sa]
   _____

7. **노래**
   [no-rae]
   _____

8. **노력**
   [no-ryeok]
   _____

9. **동의**
[dong-ui]

_____

10. **인정**
[in-jeong]

_____

11. **후회**
[hu-hoe]

_____

12. **운동**
[un-dong]

_____

13. **사랑**
[sa-rang]

_____

14. **말**
[mal]

_____

15. **생각**
[saeng-gak]

_____

Section II - Comprehension

Turn the nouns from the Vocabulary section into 하다 verbs and write the defi-
nition.
[ha-da]

1a.

_____

2a.

_____

3a.

_____

4a.

_____

5a.

_____

6a.

_____

7a.

_____

8a.

_____

9a.

_____

10a.

_____

11a.

_____

12a.

_____

13a.

_____

14a.

_____

15a.

_____

Section III – Dictation

Listen to the corresponding MP3 file. Repeat aloud what you hear, and then write it down. Each word/phrase will be said twice.

16. Track 64:

17. Track 65:

18. Track 66:

Section I - Vocabulary

Please define/translate each word or phrase in English. Then write it in your preferred language!

1. 똑똑똑
   [ttok-ttok-ttok]
   _____

2. 누구
   [nu-gu]
   _____

3. 여보세요?
   [yeo-bo-se-yo?]
   _____

4. 치즈
   [chi-jeu]
   _____

5. 사다
   [sa-da]
   _____

6. 오다
   [o-da]
   _____

7. 팔다
   [pal-da]
   _____

8. 옮기다
   [om-gi-da]
   _____

9. 전화하다
   [jeo-nwa-ha-da]
   _____

10. 만들다
    [man-deul-da]
    _____

Section II - Unscramble and Write

11. 했어가요누?
    [hae-sseo-ga-yo-nu]

    _____

12. 요구예누?
    [yo-gu-ye-nu]

    _____

13. 가전했어누화요?
    [ga-jeon-hae-sseo-nu-hwa-yo]

    _____

Section III - Comprehension

True/False

14. Saying "누구세요?" when you answer the phone is kind of rude in Korean,
    [nu-gu-se-yo?]
but it is perfectly appropriate when you answer the door. _____

15. When you are saying "who" as the subject of an action in Korean, such as in
"Who took my money?," you do not need a subject marker, you only need to use
누구. _____
[nu-gu]

16. "누구" isn't pronounced in Korean like the way you would say it in English,
[nu-gu]
rather you must put your tongue between your teeth like "th", but vocalize the
"n" sound. _____

Complete the scenario
Using the prompts, fill in the blanks with the appropriate phrase for that situation.

17. Someone knocks on the door of your office, and your co-worker goes out to
see who it is. After talking to that person for a while, your co-worker comes
back to the office alone. What can you say to your co-worker to find out who the
person was who knocked on the door?

(   )?

18. Answering the door :

A: *똑똑똑*
[*ttok-ttok-ttok*]

B: (   )?

A: 저는 현우예요.
[jeo-neun hyeo-nu-ye-yo]

19. A friend has given you a handmade gift, but you want to know who made it,
so you ask :
*(만들다) (   )?
[man-deul-da]

Section IV - Dictation

Listen to the corresponding MP3 file. Repeat aloud what you hear, and then write it down. Each word/phrase will be said twice.

20. Track 67:

21. Track 68:

22. Track 69:

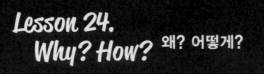

Lesson 24.
Why? How? 왜? 어떻게?

Section I - Vocabulary

Match each Korean word to its most common English translation.

1. 뭐
    [mwo]

2. 어디
    [eo-di]

3. 언제
    [eon-je]

4. 찾다
    [chat-da]

5. 오다
    [o-da]

6. 전화하다
    [jeo-nwa-ha-da]

7. 내다
    [nae-da]

8. 자주
    [ja-ju]

9. 크다
    [keu-da]

a. to come

b. when

c. where

d. to make a telephone call

e. often; frequently

f. to be big

g. what

h. to look/search for; to find

i. to pay

Talk To Me In Korean Workbook

10. **무겁다**
[mu-geop-da]

j. how

11. **의문사**
[ui-mun-sa]

k. how much + adj./adv.

12. **누구**
[nu-gu]

l. who

13. **얼마**
[eol-ma]

m. why

14. **왜**
[wae]

n. how much (money)

15. **어떻게**
[eo-tteo-ke]

o. interrogatives

16. **얼마나**
[eol-ma-na]

p. to be heavy

Section II - Translation Practice

Translate the following English sentences to Korean.

17. How did you find this? =

18. Why didn't you come yesterday? =

19. How much did you pay? =

20. How often do you come here? =

21. Why is this heavy? =

Section III - Reading Comprehension

Read each conversation and answer each question in English, and/or your pre-ferred language.

Conversation 1

A: 저기요. 그거 얼마였어요?
[jeo-gi-yo. geu-geo eol-ma-yeo-sseo-yo?]

B: 이 가방이요? 12,000원이었어요. 왜요?
[i ga-bang-i-yo? ma-ni-cheo-nwo-ni-eo-sseo-yo. wae-yo?]

A: 너무 귀여워요!
[neo-mu gwi-yeo-wo-yo!]

22. How much did Person B pay for the bag?

23. Why does Person A want to know how much the bag is?

Conversation 2

경은: 현우 씨, 왜 전화했어요?
[hyeo-noo ssi, wae jeo-nwa-hae-sseo-yo?]

현우: 어디 갔다 왔어요? 기다렸어요.
[eo-di gat-da wa-sseo-yo? gi-da-ryeo-sseo-yo.]

경은: 사무실 갔다 왔어요.
[sa-mu-sil gat-da wa-sseo-yo.]

24. Why did 현우 call 경은?
      [hyeo-nu]   [gyeong-eun]

25. Where has 경은 been?
                [gyeong-eun]

Section IV - Dictation

Listen to the corresponding MP3 file. Repeat aloud what you hear, and then write it down. Each word/phrase will be said twice.

26. Track 70:

27. Track 71:

28. Track 72:

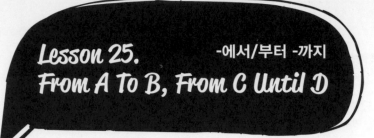

Lesson 25.
From A To B, From C Until D

-에서/부터 -까지

Section I - Vocabulary

1. "Seoul" is spelled (   ) in Hangeul.

    a. 소울
       [so-ul]
    b. 제주도
       [je-ju-do]
    c. 서울
       [seo-ul]
    d. 솔
       [sol]

2. The Korean word for "morning" is:

    a. 밤
       [bam]
    b. 아침
       [a-chim]
    c. 전화
       [jeo-nwa]
    d. 머리
       [meo-ri]

3. "부산" translates to (   ) in English:

    a. Seoul

    b. Busan

    c. Daeju

    d. Jeju Island

4. Which of the following is the Korean word for "head"?

    a. **머리**
       [meo-ri]

    b. **발**
       [bal]

    c. **허리**
       [heo-ri]

    d. **발끝**
       [bal-kkeut]

5. The word for "now" in Korean is...

    a. **내일**
       [nae-il]

    b. **언제**
       [eon-je]

    c. **여기**
       [yeo-gi]

    d. **지금**
       [ji-geum]

6. "**저녁**" in Korean means (   ) in English.
   [jeo-nyeok]

    a. Morning

    b. Afternoon

    c. Evening

    d. Night

Section II - Comprehension
Fill-in-the-blank

7. Generally you use -**에서** when talking about (   ).
                [-e-seo]

8. -부터 is most associated with (   ).
    [-bu-teo]

9. -까지 has the meaning of (   ).
    [-kka-ji]

All statements are false. Correct the underlined word or phrase to make the statement correct.

10. "-에서" and "-부터" are never interchangeable.
     [-e-seo]   [-bu-teo]

     ≫

11. "-에서" and "-부터" mean "to" or "until."
     [-e-seo]   [-bu-teo]

     ≫

12. 아침에서 저녁까지
     [a-chi-me-seo jeo-nyeok-kka-ji]

     ≫

13. 지금에서
     [ji-geu-me-seo]

     ≫

Section III - Writing
Write the following sentences in Korean

14. From home to the office =

15. From now until tomorrow =

16. Until when? =

17. From what time to what time =

18. I came from Busan. =

19. From Sweden to Seoul, it is 7,429 kilometers. *Sweden = 스웨덴

    =

Section IV - Dictation

Listen to the corresponding MP3 file. Repeat aloud what you hear, and then write it down. Each word/phrase will be said twice.

20.   Track 73:

21.   Track 74:

22.   Track 75:

Answer Key
for
TTMIK
Workbook
Level 1

Answer Key

Lesson 1

Section I – Vocabulary

1. Polite/formal language

2. Well-being; peace; health

3. you do...?; do you...?; please do...

4. Hello/Hi/How are you?/Good afternoon/
Good evening...etc.

5. Appreciation; thankfulness; gratefulness

6. I do...; I am doing...

7. Thank you/I am grateful/I am thankful/ I ap-
preciate it.

Section II - Writing practice

N/A

Section III - Comprehension

20. 안녕하세요
[an-nyeong-ha-se-yo]

21. 안녕하세요 / 안녕하세요
[an-nyeong-ha-se-yo] / [an-nyeong-ha-se-yo]

22. 존댓말
[jon-daen-mal]

23. 감사합니다
[gam-sa-ham-ni-da]

24. Period (.)/question mark (?)

Section IV - Dictation

25. 안녕하세요
[an-nyeong-ha-se-yo]

26. 존댓말
[jon-daen-mal]

27. 감사합니다
[gam-sa-ham-ni-da]

28. 안녕
[an-nyeong]

Lesson 2

Section I - Vocabulary

1. h

2. c

3. e

4. a

5. d

6. g

7. b

8. f

Section II - Comprehension

9. 네
[ne]

10. 아니요
[a-ni-yo]

11. 네, 맞아요
[ne, ma-ja-yo]

12. 존댓말
[jon-daen-mal]

Section III - Dictation

13. 아니요.
[a-ni-yo.]

14. 네, 맞아요.
[ne, ma-ja-yo.]

15. 네?
[ne?]

Section IV - Writing Practice

N/A

Lesson 3

Section I - Vocabulary

1. b

2. b

3. c

4. d

5. d

Section II - Unscramble and Write

6. 안녕하세요.
[an-nyeong-ha-se-yo.]

7. 감사합니다.
[gam-sa-ham-ni-da.]

8. 안녕히 가세요.
[an-nyeong-hi ga-se-yo.]

9. 안녕히 계세요.
[an-nyeong-hi gye-se-yo.]

Section III - Comprehension

10. d

11. c

12. c

13. a,b,c,or d

14. b

Section IV - Writing Practice

N/A

Section V - Dictation

18. 안녕히 계세요.
[an-nyeong-hi gye-se-yo.]

19. 안녕히 가세요.
[an-nyeong-hi ga-se-yo.]

20. 안녕하세요.
[an-nyeong-ha-se-yo.]

Lesson 4

Section I – Vocabulary

1. appreciation or thankfulness

2. I do; I am doing

3. apology; being sorry; feeling ashamed

4. I am sorry; I apologize

5. "Excuse me" when you want to get some-one's attention, let them know something, and/or when you want to call the waiter in a restaurant or cafe to order something.

6. Literally "just a second."

7. Literally "just a second."

Section II - Comprehension
*Answers will vary

*8. 합니다 sounds like "ham-ni-da" because when you say the 합, your mouth is already
[hap]
closed in the "m" position. Without articulat-ing the "p" in 합, you naturally move forward
[hap]
and say "니", making it sound like "ham-ni-
[ni]
da" instead of "hap-ni-da." It's too much work for the mouth to actually pronounce the "p" in 합 right before the 니.
[hap]   [ni]

OR

The "p" sound in 합, by itself, is a voiceless
[hap]
bilabial stop. However, when combined with the 니, of which "n" is an alveolar nasal
[ni]
consonant, the two of them together make a voiced bilabial nasal stop, or an "m" sound.

9.

#1 - When you want to get someone's at-tention and talk to them, or let them know something.

#2 - When you want to call upon the waiter in a restaurant or a cafe to order something.

10. No, you cannot. 죄송합니다 does not
[joe-song-ham-ni-da]
have a general meaning in Korean; it only means "I apologize", "It was my bad", "excuse me", or "I shouldn't have done that".

11. #1 - 잠시만요.
   [jam-si-man-nyo.]

   #2 - 죄송합니다.
   [joe-song-ham-ni-da.]

   #3 - 잠깐만요.
   [jam-kkan-man-nyo.]

12. c

Section III - Dictation

13. 저기요.
   [jeo-gi-yo.]

14. 죄송합니다.
   [joe-song-ham-ni-da.]

15. 잠시만요.
   [jam-si-man-nyo.]

16. 잠깐만요.
   [jam-kkan-man-nyo.]

Section IV

N/A

Lesson 5

Section I - Vocabulary

1. bag

2. water

3. office

4. school

5. I/me

6. what

Section II - Translation and Writing Practice

7. 가방이에요.
   [ga-bang-i-e-yo.]

8. 뭐예요?
   [mwo-ye-yo?]

9. 저예요.
   [jeo-ye-yo.]

10. 물이에요?
   [mu-ri-e-yo?]

11. 사무실이에요.
   [sa-mu-si-ri-e-yo.]

Section III - Comprehension

12. -이에요
   [-i-e-yo]

13. -예요
   [-ye-yo]

14. to be

15. False

16. False

17. True

18. N/A

19. True

20. False

Section IV- Dictation

21. 물이에요.
   [mu-ri-e-yo.]

22. 학교예요.
   [hak-gyo-ye-yo.]

23. 저예요.
   [jeo-ye-yo.]

24. 뭐예요?
   [mwo-ye-yo?]

Lesson 6

Section I - Vocabulary

1. c

2. e

3. g

4. b

5. f

6. a

7. d

Section II - Comprehension

8. d

9. a

10. e

11. c

12. b

Section III - Writing

N/A

Section IV - Dictation

13. 이거 책이에요.
[i-geo chae-gi-e-yo.]

14. 이거 뭐예요?
[i-geo mwo-ye-yo?]

15. 이거 물이에요.
[i-geo mu-ri-e-yo.]

16. 이거 카메라예요.
[i-geo ka-me-ra-ye-yo.]

Lesson 7

Section I - Vocabulary

1. d

2. a

3. b

4. f

5. e

6. c

Section II – Comprehension

7. 그
[geu]

8. 이
[i]

9. 저
[jeo]

Section III - Writing

10. 저 핸드폰
[jeo haen-deu-pon]

11. 그 카메라
[geu ka-me-ra]

12. 이 책
[i chaek]

13. 이 가방
[i ga-bang]

14. 저 학교
[jeo hak-gyo]

15. 그 사무실
[geu sa-mu-sil]

Lesson 8

Section I - Vocabulary

1. milk

2. water

3. cat

4. student

5. hat, cap

6. thing

7. to be not, it is not, you are not

8. this

9. It, that

10. That (over there)

Section II - Translation practice

11. 안녕하세요.
[an-nyeong-ha-se-yo.]

12. 저거 고양이 아니에요.
[jeo-geo go-yang-i a-ni-e-yo.]

13. 감사합니다.
[gam-sa-ham-ni-da]

14. 이거 커피 아니에요.
[i-geo keo-pi a-ni-e-yo.]

15. 네, (저) 학생이에요.
[ne, (jeo) hak-saeng-i-e-yo.]

16. 안녕히 가세요!
[an-nyeong-hi ga-se-yo!]

17. 이거 뭐예요?
[i-geo mwo-ye-yo?]

18. 아니요. 이거 사무실이에요.
[a-ni-yo. i-geo sa-mu-si-ri-e-yo.]

19. 그거 핸드폰 아니에요.
[geu-geo haen-deu-pon a-ni-e-yo.]

20. 네, 맞아요. 이거 우유예요.
[ne, ma-ja-yo. i-geo u-yu-ye-yo.]

Section III - Comprehension

21. d

22. c

23. b

24. a

Section IV - Dictation

25. 저 아니에요.
[jeo a-ni-e-yo.]

26. 물 아니에요.
[mul a-ni-e-yo.]

27. 이거 모자 아니에요.
[i-geo mo-ja a-ni-e-yo.]

28. 그거 우유 아니에요.
[geu-geo u-yu a-ni-e-yo.]

Lesson 9

Section I - Vocabulary

1. c

2. d

3. a

4. c

5. d

6. a

7. c

8. b

Section II - Writing practice

9. 저는
[jeo-neun]

10. 오렌지 주스는
[o-ren-ji ju-seu-neun]

11. 내일은
[nae-i-reun]

12. 가방은
[ga-bang-eun]

13. 물이
[mu-ri]

14. 학교가
[hak-gyo-ga]

15. 고양이가
[go-yang-i-ga]

16. 사무실이
[sa-mu-si-ri]

Section III - Comprehension

17. 오늘은 날씨 좋네요.
[o-neu-reun nal-ssi jot-ne-yo.]

18. 오늘 날씨는 좋네요.
[o-neul nal-ssi-neun jot-ne-yo.]

19. 이 책은 좋아요.
[i chae-geun jo-a-yo.]

20. 이 책이 좋아요.
[i chae-gi jo-a-yo.]

Lesson 10

Section I - Vocabulary

1. friend

2. time

3. fun

4. water

5. to not exist; does not exist; to not have

6. to exist; to have

Section II - Comprehension

*Answers may vary.

7. 네. 친구 있어요.
   [ne. chin-gu i-sseo-yo.]

   or

   아니요. 친구 없어요.
   [a-ni-yo. chin-gu eop-sseo-yo.]

8. 네. TTMIK 재미있어요.
   [ne. TTMIK jae-mi-i-sseo-yo.]

   or

   아니요. TTMIK 재미없어요.
   [a-ni-yo. TTMIK jae-mi-eop-sseo-yo.]

9. 시간은 없어요.
   [si-ga-neun eop-sseo-yo.]

10. 시간이 없어요.
    [si-ga-ni eop-sseo-yo.]

11. 친구는 없어요.
    [chin-gu-neun eop-sseo-yo.]

12. -이에요 = to be (something)
    [-i-e-yo]

    - This is ... ; I am ... .

    있어요 = to be; to exist (in a certain

    place), to have

    - I have ...; I'm here; It's over there

13. 아니에요 = to be not (something)
    [a-ni-e-yo]

    - This is not ...; It is not ...; I am not ...

    없어요 = to not exist, does not exist, to

not have

- You don't have ...?; I do not have...;

... does not exist

Section III - Dictation

14. 물은 있어요.
    [mu-reun i-sseo-yo.]

15. 내일은 시간 없어요.
    [nae-i-reun si-gan eop-sseo-yo.]

16. 친구는 있어요.
    [chin-gu-neun i-sseo-yo.]

Lesson 11

Section I - Vocabulary

1. f

2. g

3. a

4. j

5. i

6. h

7. d

8. b

9. e

10. c

Section II - Practice exercises

11. 없어요
    [eop-sseo-yo]

12. 있어요
    [i-sseo-yo]

13. 없어요, 주세요
    [eop-sseo-yo] [ju-se-yo]

14. 저기요. 커피 주세요.
    [jeo-gi-yo. keo-pi ju-se-yo.]

15. 오렌지 있어요?
    [o-ren-ji i-sseo-yo?]

Answer Key

Section III - Comprehension

16. a

17. b

18. b

19. c

20. a

21. d

22. d

23. e

Section IV - Dictation

24. 아이스크림 주세요.
[a-i-seu-keu-rim ju-se-yo.]

25. 커피 없어요?
[keo-pi eop-sseo-yo?]

26. 밥 주세요.
[bap ju-se-yo.]

27. 장갑 있어요?
[jang-gap i-sseo-yo?]

Lesson 12

Section I - Vocabulary

1. Kimbap - a popular Korean dish made of steamed rice and various vegetables and meat rolled in seaweed, or 김
[gim]

2. Taste

3. Well (adv.)

4. Cake

5. What

6. Oysters

7. Fried chicken

8. Samgyeopsal - Korean barbecue; thick, fatty slices of pork belly meat similar to uncured bacon

Section II - Writing practice

N/A

Section III - Comprehension

14. False - 잘 먹었습니다.
[jal meo-geo-sseum-ni-da.]

15. True

16. False - 맛
[mat]

17. False - 이 케이크 맛있어요.
[i ke-i-keu ma-si-sseo-yo.]

18. False - ma-si-sseo-yo

19. True

20. True

Section IV - Dictation

21. 삼겹살 맛있어요.
[sam-gyeop-sal ma-si-sseo-yo.]

22. 치킨 맛있어요.
[chi-kin ma-si-sseo-yo.]

23. 잘 먹었습니다.
[jal meo-geo-sseum-ni-da.]

24. 잘 먹겠습니다.
[jal meok-ge-sseum-ni-da.]

Lesson 13

Section I - Vocabulary

1. e

2. g

3. b

4. f

5. c

6. a

7. d

Section II - Writing

8. 먹고 싶어요.
[meok-go si-peo-yo.]

9. 가고 싶어요.
[ga-go si-peo-yo.]

10. 보고 싶어요.
[bo-go si-peo-yo.]

11. 맛있어요.
[ma-si-sseo-yo.]

12. 잘 먹겠습니다.
[jal meok-ge-sseum-ni-da.]

13. 더 주세요.
[deo ju-se-yo.]

14. 더 먹고 싶어요!
[deo meok-go si-peo-yo!]

Section III - Comprehension

15. I miss you

16. 다
[da]

17. 더 먹고 싶어요.
[deo meok-go si-peo-yo.]

Section IV - Dictation

18. 햄버거 먹고 싶어요.
[haem-beo-geo meok-go si-peo-yo.]

19. 회 먹고 싶어요.
[hoe meok-go si-peo-yo.]

20. 뭐 먹고 싶어요?
[mwo meok-go si-peo-yo?]

Lesson 14

Section I - Vocabulary

1. to do

2. to see

3. to eat

4. to buy

5. to drink

6. what

7. TV; television

8. to read

9. to sleep

10. to hang out; to play

11. to rest

12. to work

Section II - Comprehension

13. 네. 텔레비전 보고 싶어요.
[ne. tel-le-bi-jeon bo-go si-peo-yo.]

= Yes. I want to watch TV.

14. 이거 모자예요.
[i-geo mo-ja-ye-yo.]

= This is a hat.

15. 케이크 먹고 싶어요.
[ke-i-keu meok-go si-peo-yo.]

= I want to eat some cake.

16. 뉴스 보고 싶어요.
[nyu-seu bo-go si-peo-yo.]

= I want to watch the news.

17. 네. 더 마시고 싶어요.
[ne. deo ma-si-go si-peo-yo.]

= Yes. I want to drink more.

18. 놀고 싶어요.
[nol-go si-peo-yo.]

= I want to hang out/play.

Section III - Dictation

19. 뭐 하고 싶어요?
[mwo ha-go si-peo-yo?]

20. 쉬고 싶어요.
[swi-go si-peo-yo.]

21. 영화 보고 싶어요.
[yeong-hwa bo-go si-peo-yo.]

Answer Key

Lesson 15

Section I - Vocabulary

1. j
2. g
3. b
4. h
5. k
6. d
7. c
8. e
9. l
10. i
11. a
12. f

Section II - Writing

13. 오십사
    [o-sip-sa]
14. 구십팔
    [gu-sip-pal]
15. 육십칠
    [yuk-sip-chil]
16. 십일
    [si-bil]
17. 이십사
    [i-sip-sa]
18. 백
    [baek]
19. 오백칠십사
    [o-baek-chil-sip-sa]
20. 삼백사십삼
    [sam-baek-sa-sip-sam]
21. 구백구십구
    [gu-baek-gu-sip-gu]
22. 백이십삼
    [bae-gi-sip-sam]
23. 천
    [cheon]

24. 사천삼백구십이
    [sa-cheon-sam-baek-gu-si-bi]
25. 육천팔백십오
    [yuk-cheon-pal-baek-si-bo]
26. 구천구백구십구
    [gu-cheon-gu-baek-gu-sip-gu]
27. 칠천팔백이십구
    [chil-cheon-pal-bae-gi-sip-gu]

Section III - Dictation

28. 007
29. 8055
30. 602

Lesson 16

Section I - Vocabulary

1. to go
2. to eat
3. to sleep
4. to hit
5. to laugh
6. to hang out; to play
7. to be seen; to be visible
8. to work
9. office
10. money

Section II - Comprehension

11. ㅏ, ㅗ
12. 하
    [ha]
13. 해요
    [hae-yo]
14. ㅏ, ㅗ

15. 해요
[hae-yo]

16. 보아요
[bo-a-yo]

17. 존댓말
[jon-daen-mal]

Section III - Writing

18. 놀아요
[no-ra-yo]

19. 웃어요
[u-seo-yo]

20. 없어요
[eop-sseo-yo]

21. 와요
[wa-yo]

22. 받아요
[ba-da-yo]

23. 살아요
[sa-ra-yo]

Section IV - Dictation

24. 먹어요
[meo-geo-yo]

25. 보여요
[bo-yeo-yo]

26. 해요
[hae-yo]

Lesson 17

Section I - Vocabulary

1. to be cool; to be awesome

2. to be strange

3. to wait

4. to write; to use

5. to play; to hang out

6. to sell

7. to eat

8. to do

9. to write down

10. to come

11. to buy

Section II - Fill in the chart

12. 잡다
[jap-da]

잡아요
[ja-ba-yo]

잡았어요
[ja-ba-sseo-yo]

13. 먹다
[meok-da]

먹어요
[meo-geo-yo]

먹었어요
[meo-geo-sseo-yo]

14. 팔다
[pal-da]

팔아요
[pa-ra-yo]

팔았어요
[pa-ra-sseo-yo]

15. 쓰다
[sseu-da]

써요
[sseo-yo]

썼어요
[sseo-sseo-yo]

16. 기다리다
[gi-da-ri-da]

기다려요
[gi-da-ryeo-yo]

기다렸어요
[gi-da-ryeo-sseo-yo]

17. 이상하다
[i-sang-ha-da]

이상해요
[i-sang-hae-yo]

이상했어요
[i-sang-hae-sseo-yo]

18. 놀다
[nol-da]

놀아요
[no-ra-yo]

놀았어요
[no-ra-sseo-yo]

19. 하다
[ha-da]

해요
[hae-yo]

했어요
[hae-sseo-yo]

20. 사다
[sa-da]

사요
[sa-yo]

샀어요
[sa-sseo-yo]

21. 오다
[o-da]

와요
[wa-yo]

왔어요
[wa-sseo-yo]

22. 멋있다
[meo-sit-da]

멋있어요
[meo-si-sso-yo]

멋있었어요
[meo-si-sseo-sseo-yo]

Section III - Comprehension

23. False - final -다

24. True

25. False - 였어요
[yeo-sseo-yo]

26. False - 먹었어요
[meo-geo-sseo-yo]

Section IV - Dictation

27. 왔어요
[wa-sseo-yo]

28. 잡았어요
[ja-ba-sseo-yo]

29. 기다렸어요
[gi-da-ryeo-sseo-yo]

Lesson 18

Section I - Vocabulary

1. c

2. b

3. d

4. a

5. d

6. b

7. c

8. d

Section II - Writing

9. 에 / Where do you want to go?
[e]

10. 에 / I'm going home.
[e]

11. 에서 / I work at the office
[e-seo]

12. 에 / Where are you now?
[e]

13. 에서 / I saw my friend at school today.
[e-seo]

Section III - Comprehension

14. Person B is going to school.

15. Person B will read a book.

16. school

17. the office

Section IV - Dictation

18. 한국에 왔어요.
[han-gu-ge wa-sseo-yo.]

19. 어디에 가고 싶어요?
[eo-di-e ga-go si-peo-yo?]

20. 집에서 일해요.
[ji-be-seo i-rae-yo.]

Lesson 19

Section I - Vocabulary

1. to arrive
2. to get up
3. today
4. yesterday
5. tomorrow
6. now
7. earlier (today); a while ago (today)
8. later

Section II - Comprehension

9. 어디
   [eo-di]
10. 언제, yesterday
    [eon-je]

Section III - Writing

*Answers may vary.

N/A

Section IV - Dictation

21. 아침에 언제 일어나요?
    [a-chi-me eon-je i-reo-na-yo?]
22. 언제 집에 가요?
    [eon-je ji-be ga-yo?]

Lesson 20

Section I - Vocabulary

1. d
2. i
3. j
4. k
5. g
6. l

7. c
8. b
9. e
10. f
11. h
12. a

Section II - Comprehension

33: 삼십삼 / 서른셋
[sam-sip-sam] / [seo-reun-set]

100: 백 / 백
[baek] / [baek]

80: 팔십 / 여든
[pal-sip] / [yeo-deun]

96: 구십육 / 아흔여섯
[gu-sim-nyuk] / [a-heun-nyeo-seot]

71: 칠십일 / 일흔하나
[chil-si-bil] / [i-reu-na-na]

20: 이십 / 스물
[i-sip] / [seu-mul]

92: 구십이 / 아흔둘
[gu-si-bi] / [a-heun-dul]

68: 육십팔 / 예순여덟
[yuk-sip-pal] / [ye-sun-nyeo-deol]

11: 십일 / 열하나
[si-bil] / [yeo-ra-na]

44: 사십사 / 마흔넷
[sa-sip-sa] / [ma-heun-net]

1004: 천사 / 천넷
[cheon-sa] / [cheon-net]

Section III - Let's Count!

13. 둘 or 두 사람 or 두 명
[dul/du sa-ram/du myeong]

14. 다섯 or 다섯 개
[da-seot/da-seot gae]

15. 하나 or 한 마리
[ha-na/han ma-ri]

Section IV - Dictation

16. 808

17. 7

18. 50

Lesson 21

Section I - Vocabulary

1. to throw away

2. to be spicy

3. to eat

4. to be hungry

5. to go

6. to hurt; to be sick

7. home; house

8. yet

Section II - Comprehension

9. Using the negative verb ending, -지 않다

10. Adding 안 before a verb

11. 아니요. (김밥이) 안 매워요.
[a-ni-yo. (gim-bba-bi) an mae-wo-yo.]

12. 아니요. (케이크) 안 먹었어요.
[a-ni-yo. (ke-i-keu) an meo-geo-sseo-yo.]

13. 아니요. (집에) 안 가요.
[a-ni-yo. (ji-be) an ga-yo.]

14. 아니요. (그거) 안 버렸어요.
[a-ni-yo. (geu-geo) an beo-ryeo-sseo-yo.]

15. 아니요. 안 아파요.
[a-ni-yo. an a-pa-yo.]

Section III - Fill in the chart

16. 마시다
[ma-si-da]

안 마셔요
[an ma-syeo-yo]

마시지 않아요
[ma-si-ji a-na-yo]

17. 먹다
[meok-da]

안 먹어요
[an meo-geo-yo]

먹지 않아요
[meok-ji a-na-yo]

18. 버리다
[beo-ri-da]

안 버려요
[an beo-ryeo-yo]

버리지 않아요
[beo-ri-ji a-na-yo]

19. 아프다
[a-peu-da]

안 아파요
[an a-pa-yo]

아프지 않아요
[a-peu-ji a-na-yo]

20. 일어나다
[i-reo-na-da]

안 일어나요
[an i-reo-na-yo]

일어나지 않아요
[i-reo-na-ji a-na-yo]

21. 자다
[ja-da]

안 자요
[an ja-yo]

자지 않아요
[ja-ji a-na-yo]

22. 놀다
[nol-da]

안 놀아요
[an no-ra-yo]

놀지 않아요
[nol-ji a-na-yo]

23. 하다
[ha-da]

안 해요
[an hae-yo]

하지 않아요
[ha-ji a-na-yo]

24. 사다
sa-da]

안 사요
[an sa-yo]

사지 않아요
[sa-ji a-na-yo]

25. 보다
[bo-da]

안 봐요
[an bwa-yo]

보지 않아요
[bo-ji a-na-yo]

26. 멋있다
[meo-sit-da]

안 멋있어요
[an meo-si-sseo-yo]

멋있지 않아요
[meo-sit-ji a-na-yo]

Section IV - Dictation

27. 안 매워요?
[an mae-wo-yo?]

28. 아직 안 버렸어요.
[a-jik an beo-ryeo-sseo-yo.]

29. 집에 안 가요?
[ji-be an ga-yo?]

Lesson 22

Section I - Vocabulary

1. studying

2. work; job

3. memory

4. cleaning

5. cooking; dish

6. moving

7. song

8. effort

9. agreement; agreeing

10. admitting; acknowledgement

11. regret

12. exercise

13. love

14. words; language

15. thought; idea

Section II - Comprehension

1a. 공부하다 = to study
[gong-bu-ha-da]

2a. 일하다 = to work
[i-ra-da]

3a. 기억하다 = to remember
[gi-eo-ka-da]

4a. 청소하다 = to clean
[cheong-so-ha-da]

5a. 요리하다 = to cook
[yo-ri-ha-da]

6a. 이사하다 = to move;
[i-sa-ha-da]
          to move into a different house

7a. 노래하다 = to sing
[no-rae-ha-da]

8a. 노력하다 = to make an effort; to try hard
[no-ryeo-ka-da]

9a. 동의하다 = to agree
[dong-ui-ha-da]

10a. 인정하다 = to admit
[in-jeong-ha-da]

11a. 후회하다 = to regret
[hu-hoe-ha-da]

12a. 운동하다 = to exercise; to work out
[un-dong-ha-da]

13a. 사랑하다 = to love
[sa-rang-ha-da]

14a. 말하다 = to speak
[ma-ra-da]

15a. 생각하다 = to think
[saeng-ga-ka-da]

Section III - Dictation

16. 노력했어요.
[no-ryeo-kae-sseo-yo.]

17. 운동해요.
[un-dong-hae-yo.]

18. 노력 안 해요.
[no-ryeok an hae-yo.]

Answer Key

Lesson 23

Section I - Vocabulary

1. onomatopoeia for knocking on the door -
"knock, knock, knock"

2. who

3. [when you pick up the phone] Hello?

4. cheese

5. to buy

6. to come

7. to sell

8. to move

9. to call; to make a phone call

10. to make

Section II - Unscramble and Write

11. 누가 했어요?
[nu-ga hae-sseo-yo?]

12. 누구예요?
[nu-gu-ye-yo?]

13. 누가 전화했어요?
[nu-ga jeo-nwa-hae-sseo-yo?]

Section III - Comprehension

14. True

15. False

16. True

17. 누구예요?
[nu-gu-ye-yo?]

   or 누구였어요?
[nu-gu-yeo-sseo-yo?]

18. 누구세요?
[nu-gu-se-yo?]

19. (casual)누가 만들었어?
[nu-ga man-deu-reo-sseo?]

   or (polite)누가 만들었어요?
[nu-ga man-deu-reo-sseo-yo?]

Section IV - Dictation

20. 누구
[nu-gu]

21. 누가 왔어요?
[nu-ga wa-sseo-yo?]

22. 누가 샀어요?
[nu-ga sa-sseo-yo?]

Lesson 24

Section I - Vocabulary

1. g

2. c

3. b

4. h

5. a

6. d

7. i

8. e

9. f

10. p

11. o

12. l

13. n

14. m

15. j

16. k

Section II - Translation Practice

17. 이거 어떻게 찾았어요?
[i-geo eo-tteo-ke cha-ja-sseo-yo?]

18. 어제 왜 안 왔어요?
[eo-je wae an wa-sseo-yo?]

19. 얼마 냈어요?
[eol-ma nae-sseo-yo?]

20. 여기 얼마나 자주 와요?
[yeo-gi eol-ma-na ja-ju wa-yo?]

21. 이거 왜 무거워요?
[i-geo wae mu-geo-wo-yo?]

Section III - Reading Comprehension

22. 12,000 won

23. Because Person A thinks it is cute.

24. Because he didn't know where she was.

25. Office.

Section IV - Dictation

26. 어떻게 찾았어요?
[eo-tteo-ke cha-ja-sseo-yo?]

27. 왜 안 왔어요?
[wae an wa-sseo-yo?]

28. 얼마나 무거워요?
[eol-ma-na mu-geo-wo-yo?]

Lesson 25

Section I - Vocabulary

1. c

2. b

3. b

4. a

5. d

6. c

Section II - Comprehension

7. locations

8. time

9. "to" or "until"

10. usually

11. "from"

12. 부터
[bu-teo]

13. 부터
[bu-teo]

Section III - Writing

14. 집에서 사무실까지
[ji-be-seo sa-mu-sil-kka-ji]

15. 지금부터 내일까지
[ji-geum-bu-teo nae-il-kka-ji]

16. 언제까지?
[eon-je-kka-ji?]

17. 몇 시부터 몇 시까지
[myeot si-bu-teo myeot si-kka-ji]

18. 저는 부산에서 왔어요.
[jeo-neun bu-sa-ne-seo wa-sseo-yo.]

19. 스웨덴에서 서울까지 7,429km (칠천사백
[seu-we-de-ne-seo seo-ul-kka-ji chil-cheon-sa-bae-

이십구 킬로미터)예요.
gi-sip-gu kil-lo-mi-teo-ye-yo.]

Section IV - Dictation

20. 여기부터 저기까지
[yeo-gi-bu-teo jeo-gi-kka-ji]

21. 집에서 회사까지 어떻게 가요?
[ji-be-seo hoe-sa-kka-ji eo-tteo-ke ga-yo?]

22. 9시부터 6시까지 일해요.
[a-hop-si-bu-teo yeo-seot-si-kka-ji i-rae-yo.]